BACKSLIDERS AND

WORLDLY CHRISTIANS

by
Rev. A.M. Hills

AUTHOR OF

The Cleansing Baptism
The Establishing Grace
Fundamental Christian Theology
Homiletics and Pastoral Theology
Life of Charles G Finney
Scriptural Holiness & Keswick Teaching Compared

SCHMUL PUBLISHING COMPANY
NICHOLASVILLE, KENTUCKY

Published by Schmul Publishing Co.
PO Box 776
Nicholasville, KY USA

Printed in the United States of America

ISBN 10: 0-88019-423-5
ISBN 13: 978-0-88019-423-5

Visit us on the Internet at www.wesleyanbooks.com, or order direct from the publisher by calling 800-772-6657, or by writing to the above address.

Contents

DEDICATION

To those who have consciously lost their first love, and realize that they have backslidden, but do not know that Jesus is waiting with infinite tenderness to restore them; and to the still larger class who are being charmed by the world and are consciously losing their hold on God, and would welcome a renewal of their strength, these pages are affectionately dedicated by,

—THE AUTHOR.

FOREWORD

REMEMBER FROM WHENCE you have fallen. You were once full of zeal for the glory of your divine Deliverer, and the salvation of those for whom He died. You could then reprove sin, and weep over and expostulate with sinners. You could deny yourself almost your necessary sleep and food, in order to promote the interests of your Redeemer's kingdom.

Where is now your zeal for the Lord of Hosts? Can you deny self, sacrifice your ease, honor, reputation, or wealth for His glory, as you once did? Remember! Compare your present state with your former one. Let conscience speak, let facts speak, and honestly admit the truth; and if you are condemned, write yourself down—backslider in heart.

Too many Christians have far too light an estimate of heart unfaithfulness. I have sometimes heard them speak of five or ten years' half-heartedness as a very light thing, slurring it over, as it were, with a very thin and superficial sort of confession.

But our Lord does not so regard it. He looks upon it as a very serious matter, a very heinous sin, a most God-dishonoring experience. So much so, that He threatens the Ephesian backsliders that unless they repent, notwithstanding all their good works, He will come unto them in judgment and remove their candlestick out of its place.

—CATHERINE BOOTH

Chapter 1
SOME FEATURES OF PETER'S BACKSLIDING

GOD PUT INTO THE MOUTH of Jeremiah the words, "My people are bent to backsliding." This has been the characteristic of man through all generations. As Moody once said, "Apart from God, we are a bad lot, the whole of us."

The children of Israel backslid under the very shadow of Sinai in sight of the pillar of fire and cloud, and under the leadership of the greatest of earth's heroes, "Moses, the man of God." They backslid again at Kadesh, on the borders of Canaan, and exhausted the patience of God. The whole generation turned back into the wilderness to die outside the Promised Land.

The revivals under Samuel and David and Elijah and Ezra are so many evidences of lapses from a former faith; and the burning messages and tears of Jeremiah and Ezekiel and Daniel stand forever as witnesses to the treachery of the human heart.

Paul complained that the Galatian believers had been bewitched to turn from the true gospel. Peter and Jude and John felt called upon to write against the "Christian Science" "seducers" of their day, and their caustic language burns like vitriol.

The purity of the early church backslid into the abominations of Roman Catholicism and the night of the Dark Ages.

The Reformation of Luther in two brief centuries declined into a formalism as confirmed, and a morality as gross, and an irreligion as dark as the Catholicism from which it had sprung. God had to raise up Wesley and his helpers to reform the Reformation.

Three months before his death John Wesley wrote to Adam Clarke, "To retain the grace of God is much more than to gain it: *hardly one in three does this.* And this should be strongly and explicitly urged on all who have tasted of perfect love." Doubtless the old man had witnessed a painful amount of backsliding among his beloved followers that called forth such a remark.

Charles G. Finney was appalled at the backsliding which followed his great revivals; and no man ever plowed deeper or taught more carefully, or did more thorough work in the line of conversion than did he. This is what led him to try to get the believers of his day sanctified and confirmed in the Christian life.

The Bishops of the M. E. Church in March 1900, issued an address to the ministers and churches calling Methodism to fasting and prayer. It bewailed the fact that "year before last our advance was checked. Last year our advanced column has been forced back a little. The lost ground is paved with the dead. Methodism was called into being to teach and illustrate the witness of the Spirit, and that to every state of grace—conviction, justification, regeneration, adoption, and sanctification... There are now unhappily many Methodists who lack present knowledge of New Testament salvation. They have slipped a cog in their experience and have to *date back to some dead experience* to find their assurance and title to Scriptural nobility. It is this slipped cog in our experience that ails our statistics." Could the backslidden condition of a whole denomination be more pathetically confessed?

Manifestly backsliding is no new thing, since the angels backslid in heaven, and our first parents in Eden; and it has continued through the generations to this hour.

We will first take the backsliding of the Apostle Peter, and his recovery for our subject. He is an interesting character, bold, energetic, impulsive, daring. He carried his heart on his sleeve, and all felt its warmth. He was a born leader of men, much like the impulsive Esau. But like other popular men, he had his weak traits. No one man is gifted with all the elements of greatness, and perhaps *leaders* have their foibles to an unusual degree. Peter had. His has been a name to conjure with. The Roman Catholic Church has built up its monstrous fabric on a misinterpreted and exaggerated passage of Scripture relative to Peter; hence her papacy and her foolish claim to universal power.

We Protestants probably think of him more frequently as he appears in that most memorable night of his life when he denied his Lord.

Of all the acts of his life, that one comes most often before the mind.

Let us consider

1. The features and circumstances of his sin. Bear in mind his more than three years of intimate companionship with Jesus. He was not a new convert to whom the voice of his Lord was scarcely yet familiar, and with whose character he was but slightly acquainted. He had been an eyewitness of a thousand of Jesus' miracles. He had heard the matchless sermons as they fell from the lips that spake as man never spake. He had heard the private conversations when the Master's heart was fully disclosed in its infinite tenderness and love. He had witnessed the awful majesty of His Godlike mien when even His enemies fell paralyzed by the look of His eye. He had seen His tears of sympathy over private grief, and heard His sobs of compassion as He wept over the doomed city of His fathers. Aye, he had seen His transparent integrity, His infinite goodness, and the radiance of His eternal glory as the voice of the Heavenly Father proclaimed, "This is my beloved Son, in whom I am well pleased."

And with all these opportunities to know his Lord,

he was blessed with quick intuitions, the discerning vision, the spiritual perception that could see and appreciate the nature of Christ. Ah, he knew Him, and had been the boldest of the twelve in his professions, and the most confident in his assertions. And yet this dark sin—he denied his Lord.

His sin was the sin of *an intimate friend*. This fact alone dips the deed in midnight darkness and paints it with blackest hue. How sacred should be the bonds of friendship, and how few are worthy to wear them! Every impulse of loyalty, every instinct of honor should have led him to be true to his Lord. How do the devotion of David and Jonathan to each other condemn his baseness! They loved with a love surpassing the love of women, and one of them hazarded his life and gave his crown to the other. But what did Peter hazard? What did he venture for the sake of his great Friend?

Think of his intimacy: he had been one of the honored three, in the heart counsels of the Lord. His eyes had been permitted to see and his ears to hear things denied to most of the other disciples, when his Master had raised the dead, and wrestled in Gethsemane, and talked with Moses and Elias just from heaven. Ah, what holy intimacy! and yet the awful sin of denial!

2. Consider the *time* of the sin.

It was in that wonderful "Passion week," when Jesus had His triumphal entry into Jerusalem; when the days were crowded with the most thrilling events in the Master's life—majestic displays of His divinity. It was the very night of the Passover, when Jesus washed the disciples' feet in more than human humility and condescension. He had seen Judas fall and betray his Lord. That of itself should have shocked him and filled his very soul with horror and driven him to his Master's bosom with renewed vows of fidelity, and fresh outpourings of love.

Yes, since the sun had set on the evening of that awful night, he had listened to the sublimest discourse that ever fell from human lips upon mortal ears. It is recorded in the fourteenth, fifteenth, and sixteenth chapters of the Gospel of John; and by the common consent of spiritual minds it is the deepest, most profoundly spiritual passage in the entire Word of God. President Dwight told us at Yale that human thought could sound no deeper depths, and human words could express no greater truths and be intelligible.

And this discourse was followed by the Intercessory Prayer in which the Son of God pleaded with the Father for the sanctification of believers of all ages, that they might be kept from evil, and bound together in love.

And before they separated they partook of the communion, the bread that represented the body of Jesus broken for sin, and the blood shed for its cleansing, a ceremony that has kindled the hearts of believers through all the ages.

From such a scene they went to the garden of Gethsemane, where the crushing burden of the world's sin pressed the sweat of blood from Jesus' body, and broke His heart. After days of such events as man had never before witnessed, on such a night, with the utterances of Jesus inspiring His soul the words of His prayer still lingering in his ear, and the groans of Gethsemane anguish moving his inmost soul, with lips still moist with the wine of the sacrament, Peter denied his Lord! Could the sin have been more aggravated?

Chapter 2
OTHER FEATURES OF PETER'S SIN

3. THE SIN WAS COMMITTED after the most explicit and immediate warnings. The temptation, therefore, could not have taken him unawares.

The strength of temptation often lies chiefly in its *suddenness*. Men are "taken unawares." The archfiend leaps upon a soul like a leopard springing from a tree upon the unsuspecting deer walking underneath. No time is given for reflection, no opportunity to marshal the forces of the soul for resistance. Before there is a chance to think, the spark is struck that explodes a magazine of powder-like passion in the unwary breast. The impulses exploded, and a deed was done that will cause a lifetime of regret. Such experiences come in every man's life, and we become sadly conscious of our frailty and utter need of God.

But Peter had no such excuse. He had the most ample and repeated warnings. At the supper Jesus said: "Simon, Simon, behold Satan asked to have you, that he might sift you as wheat: but I have made supplication for you that thy faith fail not." And Peter said unto Him: "Lord, with thee I am ready to go both to prison and to death." Jesus saith unto him: "Verily, I say unto thee that thou today, even this night before the cock crow twice thou shalt deny me thrice." But he spake exceeding vehemently, "If I must die with thee I will not deny thee." This was probably not more than three or four hours before the first denial.

Still later in the garden, Jesus said unto Peter, "Simon, sleepest thou? Couldst thou not watch one hour? Watch and pray that ye enter not into temptation."

And this loving reproof and warning was repeated. All these warnings deepen the responsibility and crimson the guilt of the awful sin.

4. The sin of Peter was aggravated by *repetition*. After such explicit warnings, *one* denial would have been sad and excuseless enough. It is inconceivable how he could have denied his Lord at all on that night. He had seen and heard so much during the last few hours, that we could have expected him to be all alert in his watchfulness. But nothing seemed to sober Peter's natural impulsiveness. He denied once! "I neither know nor understand what thou sayest. And he went out into the porch and the cock crew."

Oh, why did not its voice remind him of the warning of his Lord? How could he have failed to note the danger of his surroundings and the weakness of his heart?

But a little before Jesus had foretold him that the Shepherd would be smitten and the sheep scattered abroad: and he had vauntingly replied: "Although all shall be offended yet will not I." While this note of warning and his own boasting are yet so fresh in his soul that he cannot have forgotten, and he almost hears their lingering echoes, he *does* get offended that he ever knew Jesus, and lies about it! And he hears the cock remind him of his shame! But he still does not gather up his waning moral forces, and get hold of himself.

One such denial should have been enough to have put him on his guard, but it didn't! Instead of drawing nearer to Jesus' side, he withdraws himself and gets still farther away into the porch, and denies a second time. Still unchecked as if rushing on precipitately, with breakneck speed to determined ruin, at another taunt, "He began to curse and swear. 'I know not this man!'"

How could the fall have been worse, or more complete! How strange that the warmhearted Peter should have thus fallen! How prolific is sin! Evil thoughts grow into evil deeds. One sin begets another, and each generation the progeny becomes more base. Saul's self-will ends in Saul's suicide! Peter, fresh from the communion table, avoids reproach for Christ's sake, and in an hour or two curses and swears and denies his Lord! So sin ever sweeps on, plunges deeper and deeper until it lands the poor victim in the bottomless pit.

5. Peter, in very truth, was but slightly tempted. It

was only the twit of bystanders, the taunt of a waiting maid! He was in no danger whatever, as the
whole story shows. No violence to the disciples was
thought of for a moment by anybody. The enemies
of God only despised the poor, ignorant disciples.
They could dismiss them with a few jeers; it was *Jesus*,
the blessed Son of God, whom they, with infernal
malice, were hounding to His death.

But yet, this, too, is a common feature of sin. Men
who can go into the ranks and march against a bat-
tery of guns, will throw their good resolutions to the
winds and yield to *a banter to drink,* against every inward protest of their soul.

Men can go into the prize ring, or enter the football eleven and engage in physical contests that en-
danger limbs and are often fatal to life, and then be
as veritable cowards as ever breathed the breath of
air in the presence of a wicked social custom! Men of
large physical proportions and corresponding
strength are puling babes before the sneer of a companion. The mighty Samson who could slay a thousand men with the jawbone of an ass, threw away
his glory and broke his covenant with God, at the
teasing of a worthless woman. Oh, shame that we
should allow moral influences to break down our
spiritual manhood and womanhood when physical
influences are entirely wanting!

6. This sin was committed so *very near his Lord.*
Jesus, whom he had seen but an hour before in
Gethsemane anguish, was within sight and sound of
him. He can hear the lies of the false witnesses,

whose falseness he knows so well. Why does he not correct them? But a few hours before he said he would die for his Lord. Now his great Friend and Saviour is on trial for His life and needs witnesses. Where is Peter with his testimony?

He hears Jesus' testimony that He is the Son of God. Why does not Peter's soul kindle within him to substantiate the sublime truth? Why does he not tell what he has seen, how at a word of his Lord, lepers have been cleansed, the eyes of the blind have been opened, the ears of the deaf have been unstopped, and hungry thousands have been fed? What kept him from declaring that he had seen his Lord call forth the dead from the bier and the sepulchre, and with the voice of His omnipotence hush the angry waves of Galilee as a mother might hush the wails of a sick babe on her knee?

Jesus is being condemned to death for the sin of blasphemy because He had declared Himself to be the Son of God. Why did not Peter tell what he had seen and heard on the Mount of Transfiguration, when Moses and Elias came from heaven to talk with Christ, and there came a voice from the heavens; "This is my beloved Son, in whom I am well pleased; hear ye him!"

He sees the buffeting, the spitting of vile men into the blessed face, the infamous lashing, the derision and cruel crowning with thorns—he beholds the Godlike mien of Jesus, as He stands in divine and unresisting silence before the wretches who torment Him. Where are the noble emotions of Peter? How is it that sympathy for the suffering Master does not move him to indignant protest? Why does he not let his fainting, suffering Lord lean upon his strong arm? Why does he not wipe the accursed spittle from His face? Why does he not show a manly loyalty to the blessed Saviour in this hour of His need, when the powers of darkness are in the ascendant? Ah! why, but this, that Peter has backslidden? Sympathy, courage, friendship, love, gratitude, every holy impulse is swallowed up in the vile cowardice of a backslidden heart.

If this story had come down to us by tradition rather than in the Bible, no one could have believed it. All, all makes Peter's sin so base! Every consideration darkens the shadows and deepens the stains!

Chapter 3
STEPS THAT LED TO PETER'S DOWNFALL

IT IS DOUBTFUL if a moral fall is ever precipitous. People decline in religion and backslide *gradually*. Like descending a stairway, they go down step by step.

1. The preparation for Peter's fall was laid in his self-confidence and religious conceit. How long he had nursed it we do not know. What developed it we can only conjecture. It was painfully manifest, however, in the upper chamber when he boastfully declared, "If all shall be offended in thee, I will never be offended." It was as much as to say, "James and John may deny You; Thomas and Matthew may play the coward and desert You; all men who have followed You may yield to the opposition and desert You: but I am stronger and braver than they all. I will never do it." The Christian may well tremble who is coming into this frame of mind. But it is the very last thing he does. When a man prides himself on his strength,

and grows self-confident, he is already tottering to his fall. God has noticed it, and warns us, "Let him that thinketh he standeth take heed lest he fall." The remarkable thing about it is that very great men have fallen just where they were the strongest.

There was Moses, who was "slow of speech" and "the meekest of men"; yet, strangely enough, it was he who spoke and acted hastily, and was kept out of the promised land! It was Elijah, the bravest of the brave, after the wonderful victory of Carmel, who ran away in fear at the threat of a woman! And when such men as Moses, Elijah, and Peter fall, when tempted where they are strongest, it ought to make all ordinary mortals beware of having any confidence in self, and teach us all that our only strength is in God. In the vale of humility lies the safest path for mortals to tread.

The great Moody once told this remarkable thing about himself: "When I was first converted I used to think that when I got to be a Christian of twenty years' standing I should rejoice because there would be no danger of my falling. My friends, there is more danger of falling now than there was then. Do you know why? Because the more useful a man becomes, the better target he is for the devil. The devil is more watchful to see if he can trip him up, and the fall is a great deal more for a man that has risen to be used of God. The higher a man gets, the greater the fall. Therefore every man that is used of God ought to be very humble and keep down in the dust, or in some unguarded moment he will fall into sin."

2. Peter's over-confidence led him to go to sleep. Jesus repeatedly begged him to *"watch and pray."* The Saviour's eye foresaw the dark hour and the serious temptation just ahead. After such warnings and re-iterations of coming peril, one would have supposed that he would have watched and prayed both for himself and his grief-stricken Master. But he had such a sense of security that nothing moved him, not even the agony and bloody sweat of his Lord. The devil can do pretty much what he pleases with people who are asleep religiously. Everything is optimistic and rose-tinted then. They see no peril in worldliness; none in the theater, or the card-party; none in the dance, or in moderate drinking. Parents will lead their children into all these things, and never wake up to the evil they have wrought until the fatal charms of sin have bound them and they are fast slipping into hell. Peter was asleep, and multitudes of Christians today are just like him, fast asleep!

3. The next hour we see Peter following Jesus *afar off*. The Master has been arrested, and is being led away to trial. The sleepy disciple, in the hour of need, when he might be the most comfort to his Lord, is "following afar off" — too far away to be of any account.

Oh, how many professors of religion are just like him! In the critical hours, when they are most needed, when the cause of Jesus is suffering for the want of friends and helpers, when Jesus is being be-trayed and crucified, they are sadly wanting. They coolly stand off at a distance, like an unconcerned observer, and watch how it will go, and how the outcome will be. Such conduct is the sure prelude to a denial. The time is not distant when, in the sharp stress of some temptation, in some crisis of affairs they will deny or betray "the Lord that bought them."

4. Peter, a little later, was actually sitting *with Christ's enemies.* "O the blessedness of the man who walketh not in the counsel of the ungodly, nor standeth in the way of sinners, nor sitteth in the seat of the scornful!" It is a perilous thing when a follower of Christ gets away from the side of Jesus, and from the companionship of his fellow disciples, and finds himself surrounded by his spiritual foes. What do they care about the welfare of his soul? What interest have they in his spiritual well-being? They get amusement in tearing down his character, and delight themselves in guying him about his past piety.

Just listen to these foes of Jesus as they taunt Peter. A maid says to him, "Thou also wast with Jesus of Galilee!" "But he denied saying, Woman, I know him not." After awhile another maid provokingly points the finger at him and says, "This man was also with Jesus the Nazarene!" "And again he denied with an oath, I know not the man."

After a little while others, to increase the sport, began to say with a sneer, "Of a truth thou art one of them; for thy speech betrayeth thee!" You talk some like Jesus, you don't swear like the rest of us do. Your whole conduct shows that you are one of them!

"Then began he to curse and to swear, I know not the man!" He attempts to show them that he can blaspheme as vilely as any of them! Poor Peter, how fallen!

How many professed followers of Jesus are, like Peter, going down step by step! First, they are too self-confident to heed any warning. Second, they give up watching and prayer. Third, they follow afar off. Fourth, they get among the foes of Jesus and "sit down to warm themselves," to make a prolonged stay and find comfort among the enemies of God. What means the rage for clubs, and unions, and lodges, and orders, and guilds, and societies of every kind? How is it that husbands and fathers desert wife and children and the family altar and spend the evening until midnight behind guarded doors and blinded windows, with a band of men who have little sympathy with their aspirations and are utter strangers to their Christ? How is it that mothers who have named the name of Jesus, will turn their children over to hirelings, and spend their evenings at the theater, or the progressive euchre party, in a senseless hunt for enjoyment?

Alas! has the companionship of Jesus lost its charm? Has the service of the Master no more attraction for the heart? Can enjoyment be found no longer in doing good? If so, then Christ has already been denied, religion is dead, and the backsliding is complete. No spiritual exercise is proper for such a soul but to "go out and weep bitterly," tears of unfeigned repentance, and fall again at the Master's feet and beg for mercy.

Chapter 4
THE RECOVERY

LET US NOW CONSIDER the recovery of Peter. 1. The cause of it was not primarily in himself. Bear in mind that Jesus had foreseen it and foretold it even to Peter. He had also prayed over it, that Peter might escape the sifting of Satan and turn again to his injured Lord.

And when he fell, as the cock crowed the second time, Jesus gave Peter a look. Oh, that look! It reminded the fallen soul of what he had done. It was a look of infinite pity, the reproachful look of grieved and compassionate love!

Julius Caesar loved the visionary, fanatical Brutus as a father might love a son: and when Brutus joined with other base assassins, who wished to kill Caesar only because they envied his greatness, and drove his dagger into his body, Caesar gave Brutus a look of wounded love, and exclaimed, "And thou, too, Brutus!" That look will haunt Brutus forever.

How much more potent must have been this grieved look of the infinite Christ! Its rebuking but ineffable tenderness broke Peter's heart, "AND HE WENT OUT AND WEPT BITTERLY!"

We may pause here for a moment, to reflect upon the amazing, forgiving love of Jesus for the backslider. The language of his heart is, "How can I give thee up, O Ephraim?... My repentings are kindled together." "I am married to the backslider." "Return unto me and I will return unto you." "I will heal your backslidings. I will love you freely for my own sake."

How can the compassionate Saviour bear to see one of His redeemed disciples, who has walked with Him in the intimacy of holy friendship, to whose prayers He has listened and whose confessions of love have delighted His heart, withdraw into the camp of the enemy, and go down to sin and death? How can He bear to see those whom He has created and redeemed and taught, take their ransomed powers and serve the prince of darkness? Oh, the depth of the love that bought us! Oh, the patience of the grace that bears with us, and having loved us, loves to the end! I believe Jesus saves all whom He can, and gives us up only when He must. "A bruised reed he will not break and a smoking flax he will not quench."

2. Notice Peter wept bitter tears of repentance AT ONCE. He did not remain blind to his sin. He did not deny it, or cover it up. "If we confess our sins, he is faithful and just to forgive us our sins, and to cleanse us from all unrighteousness."

"He that covereth his transgressions shall not prosper; but whoso confesseth and forsaketh them shall obtain mercy." Jesus has "compassion on the ignorant and on them that are out of the way." Those who once blazed in their orbit of duty like a star of the first magnitude, and have since gone out in darkness, may regain their light and glory. Jesus longs for their return and will help them back. How tender the assurance, "He has compassion on them that are out of the way."

The saddest thing we see in all our rounds of Christian labor is the ease with which some who have slipped and fallen lie down in hopelessness and let the devil and his companions dance a jubilee over their downfall. It is as if they gloried in their ruin, and hugged their chains. Oh, that all who are overtaken in a fault, or have been in any way snared by Satan, would hasten back to their refuge and get under the blood! If they would only betake themselves at once in penitence and faith to their injured Saviour, they would find Him all compassion and grace. They would get restored before Satan had really secured them with his chains.

"Peter went out and wept bitterly." Of course he did. He carried a lonely and a heavy heart. Nothing could fill the void where once his Lord had been. Nothing can ever take the place of Jesus to one who has really known Him. "All substitutes for the rest and joy of an indwelling Christ are utter failures."

Peter did not persist in sinning. He abhorred his cowardice and his falsehood. He lamented his profanity. He shed the bitter tears of contrition over his base denial of his blessed Lord. He yielded to the heavenly impulse and let the look of Christ subdue his heart.

When Jesus rose from the dead He sent by Mary a special message to this poor soul: "Go tell my disciples AND PETER." He knew that Peter would be despondent and heartbroken; His infinite compassion went out toward him. He longed to draw him to His breast in forgiving love.

3. Peter *returned* to his Lord. He was fully recovered and restored. He learned a much-needed lesson from his downfall, and made of his failure a stepping-stone to better things. He was never so immodest, and never so rash again. A humility came into his soul which he had never known before. He sought and obtained the baptism with the Holy Spirit, and his "bent to backsliding" was taken away: he entered a life of consecration and service fruitful in results beyond any thing he had ever dreamed.

Peter's afterlife was worthy of his name. His character was firm as a rock: his courage was unquestioned. We see but one spot tarnishing his later life, when Paul had to rebuke him because he drew back from associating with Gentile Christians, *"fearing them that were of the circumcision."* His closing years were rich and rounded out in usefulness, and he went to a martyr's death. He was condemned to be crucified and he humbly requested that he might be crucified head downward, as he was not worthy to die like his Lord.

And thus this man, once a backslider, reached at last the glory of a martyr's crown.

Let any backslider who may ever read these lines gather hope.

He may get his lost blessing back. As Dr. Carradine beautifully says, "Let the heart-cheering truth be taken up with golden trumpets, silver bugles, beating drums, and clashing cymbals. Let some angelic voice in the sky that can be heard around the world cry out, 'Though sin abounds yet grace much more abounds,' and the whole race thunder out a hallelujah of thanksgiving, as they gather from these words the possibility of return, from all sin and spiritual loss and wandering, unto God."

We may draw some important lessons from this incident in Peter's life.

1. There is a much-needed warning to all of us who are following Jesus. Compared with the might of Satan who tempts us we are all weak. There are none of us who may not fall from the very side of Christ, from a heaven of privilege, from the communion table, and the covenant with God fresh upon our lips. There is absolutely no room for religious conceit in any human heart. "Let him that thinketh he standeth take heed lest he fall." "Watch and pray that ye enter not into temptation," is an injunction that never should be given to a Christian heart in vain.

2. But if one should fall, what then? Oh, then let the heart break and the tears of repentance flow! Abhor the sin, every feature of it, and every circumstance. Confess it honestly, and forsake it utterly.

Repentance and confession, but not remorse! Satan would have been glad to have had Peter do what Judas did. He was struck through with remorse and went out and hanged himself. It would delight all hell if, when we have fallen, we should lie down in remorse and let the hounds of despair dog us to our doom. It is not pleasing to the merciful Christ for us to distrust Him in that way. He still loves us and longs to save. He sent to us by the pen of the Apostle John this gracious message, "My little children, these things I write unto you, that ye sin not. And if any man sin, we have an advocate with the Father, Jesus Christ the righteous."

What hope the prayer of the penitent David has brought down the centuries, "A broken and a contrite heart, O God, thou wilt not despise."

3. Should any backslider hear this message or read these lines, let him learn of Peter to return to a life of deeper devotion, of warmer love, of more efficient service. What inspiration and hope come to us all from Peter's after career! He had learned that notwithstanding his love for Jesus and his new birth which he could not question, there was a dark carnality in his heart which ought not to be there. He went with his fellow disciples to the upper chamber and prayed ten days until the Pentecostal blessing came. The cleansing baptism with the Holy Spirit was poured upon him. The vaunting and vanity, the cursing and lying and cowardice and infidelity were taken out of him. In their place was given the enduement of power to preach the great sermon at

Pentecost, to work miracles, to lead the apostolic band, to carry the gospel to far-off provinces, to be a pillar of the church of Jesus Christ, until he gained a martyr's crown.

Oh, what blessed fruitfulness for a man once a sorry backslider! Let those who have fallen learn from him the lesson of hope. Let them fall before Jesus in penitence, and bathe His feet with their tears. Let them, when restored, seek the sanctifying baptism with the Holy Spirit, and then go forth to bless the fallen and be angels of mercy to men.

Chapter 5
LOT, THE WORLDLY PROFESSOR

JESUS UTTERED NO TRUTH more needed in our day than when He declared, "Ye cannot serve God and mammon." A multitude of professors of religion in all our churches are trying to do it. They seem to doubt the supreme importance of spiritual things, and to be inclined to the opinion that it pays better to be a "half-hearted Christian," getting the cream of this world, and heaven besides. In truth, these people are after both worlds. They make sure of this, and they hope not to miss the felicity of the next.

These people join the church, and call themselves Christians, but they are quick to inform us that they are not the spiritual kind. They are *paying* members rather than *praying* members, and they feel themselves indispensable to the church of Christ.

Lot is evidently a type of this class, and a study of his character and career will be profitable to us all. His whole life seems to have been tinged with earthly colorings, and to have been struck through with the spirit of the world. He preferred to live on the borderland of true Christian experience, rather than in the land itself, and to be quite a little more at home with the filthy Sodomites than with the praying household of his Uncle Abram. Alas! he was dominated by the spirit of the world!

"So Abram went, as the Lord had spoken unto him: *and Lot went with him...* and into the land of Canaan they came." So far so good, he is in a good place and in good company. But even here there may be a clue to his character. He went *with Abram* into Canaan, and then *with* him into Egypt where probably neither of them ought to have gone. God had not called Abram to go into Egypt, but into Canaan. When I entered the Holiness movement, and the trials began to come thick and fast, an old veteran said to me, "God will have a tried people!" The Lord tried Abram with a drought, and he ran off into Egypt, and fell into temptation and a sin that tarnished the beauty of his life's record. God's people would better endure trials in Canaan than run down into Egypt to escape them.

But, you notice, Lot *went with him*. What vast numbers of people are always going *with* somebody else, whether right or wrong! They never seem to stand alone, or to breast the current of circumstances, or to stand against the tide of popular opinion.

In Egypt both men got well on the way to abounding wealth. Right there many go down. With riches come peculiar temptations which few can withstand.

Covetousness, prayerlessness, worldliness usually increase with the multiplication of earthly goods. Moody observed that "wealth becomes a trouble if it is procured in Haran, or Egypt, or Sodom: it brings no blessing if God's people get it outside of Canaan." These men return to the country God had marked out for them, and the very next thing we bear is that the herdmen of the two quarrel about the water privileges or the pasturage for the vast flocks. Then the underlying principles of the two men, and their true characters, come to the surface. Abram, the elder, to whom the whole land had been promised, showed deep solicitude for the honor of God in the presence of the heathen. Whatever loss he might suffer, he would not quarrel with his nephew before them. He unselfishly waived his prior claim and greater rights, and generously offered to Lot his first choice of the whole land.

What a momentous thing is a young man's choice! It is the turn of the wheel that decides the course of the ship of life. It is the casting of the dice of destiny. In all the chemistry of the heart, there is no element so active, so manifest, and so mighty as choice. Fortunate, thrice fortunate, would it have been if this young man had been impelled by gratitude and reverence and respect to refuse the choice, instead of moved by a self-seeking impulse to make a decision absolutely fatal to his life. Yea, blessed would he have been if he had turned the whole matter over to a higher tribunal and let God decide for him! It is questionable if a follower of God has a right to make any choice vital to the life, without seeking divine guidance and making it for the glory of God.

But there is not the slightest evidence that Lot had a thought of God or his religion when he made the momentous choice that insured his ruin. This is the simple story, "Lot lifted up his eyes and beheld all the plain of Jordan, that it was well watered... So Lot chose him all the plain of Jordan: and Lot dwelt in the cities of the plain and pitched his tent toward Sodom. Now the men of Sodom were wicked and sinners against the Lord exceedingly."

Lot allowed worldly considerations alone to move him, good water, fine pastures, close to a city market, good business opportunities, and a splendid chance to make money! To be sure there was awful sin in the neighborhood! But then, he must not let little scruples like that interfere with business. Business and religion must not mix!

By just such reasoning, thousands of Christians are going down today, and are being swallowed up in a maelstrom of worldliness. They leave their souls out of account, and do not consult God when they make their temporal choices. Young men start out in life without seeking divine direction; they stay here or go there, enter this occupation or that profession to get rich, to have comfort and luxury, to be pleasantly situated, not asking counsel of Him who says, *"Seek ye first the kingdom of God and his righteousness."*

Men are so determined to carry out their ambitious schemes that all moral considerations are ignored. They choose social and business relations, their callings, professions, settlements, companionships, guided only by "the lust of the flesh, the lust of the eyes, and the pride of life," with no regard for God or the interests of their souls. Their eyes are blinded to all moral distinctions by their intense desire for material things. The glitter of gold makes them oblivious to the possible consequences of their acts, and the hope of some worldly gain silences their consciences in their protests against evil.

Lot was careless and covetous, eager to be wealthy and indifferent about spiritual things. He did not ask where God wanted him, or where it would be safe for him and his family to dwell. He thought he could manage business without prayer. This chance to make money was altogether too fine to let pass! He doubtless was one of those men who determined *"to die rich."* There are many such. I have read of one recently who "turned every stone" to accumulate wealth! All his energy and every faculty was pushed toward that one end. "Wealth, wealth, wealth! money, money, money!" was his cry, and at last it drove him mad. They took him to the insane asylum where he threw himself into a rocking chair and cried: "Millions of money, and in a madhouse!" A sorry footing up of a life's work! "They that will be rich fall into divers temptations and many snares of the devil."

No doubt Lot's new neighbors and business associates congratulated him on his wise choice. They declared that he was a shrewd and promising young fellow whose business sagacity would bring him to the front in time and make him someday worth far more than his rustic old uncle on the plains. For a time, indeed, to human vision, his choice seemed wise, and his business venture a grand success. Most people, if asked about Abram, would have said patronizingly that he was a nice old gentleman, but he was too conscientious and religious to ever make his mark in this everyday world.

Someone has quaintly observed that a man can see farther on his knees than when standing on his feet. Abram was very far-sighted. When he got on his knees night and morning, worshipping God at the altar before his tent, he could see beyond his flocks and herds, beyond Lebanon and Sodom, beyond Ur and Egypt, beyond the horizon of earthly things. He looked far away into the unseen realm and got glimpses of the "city that hath foundations, whose builder and maker is God." He was so entranced with the heavenly vision that he solemnly resolved that, whether he got much or little of earth, he would make heaven.

We find in the consequences that followed this choice of Lot an illustration of the great importance of moral tendencies. There are a great many people who are ever ready to defend a multitude of things which earnest Christians from time immemorial have been accustomed to look upon with suspicion, and regard as inexpedient and dangerous, if not actually sinful. They champion cards and the dance and the theater, and billiards and horse racing and tobacco and moderate drinking. They laugh at the idea that any should frown upon these things, and they argue that they are not a sin in themselves. Perhaps not, but let us turn to the history of Lot and learn a never-to-be-forgotten lesson. He first "lifted up his eyes and looked toward Sodom." Then he "pitched his tent *toward* (or as far as) Sodom." Now he might have argued very plausibly, and perhaps did, that the Almighty watered the plain of Jordan and caused the grass to grow there, and it certainly couldn't be wrong to permit his camels and oxen to eat it. Precisely so do men argue that the Lord caused the grapes to grow and made man with such a nature that he delights to taste their fermented juice: therefore it cannot be wrong *per se* to drink it. He made the feet of men and women, and so formed their minds, that the strains of the violin exercise a strange fascination over them and set their feet to going in rhythmic motion: therefore it cannot be a sin to dance! And by a similar process of reasoning, all the popular evils that curse society and impede the progress of the Christian religion can be defended as not necessarily sinful.

But the tendencies of acts, the probable consequences of things, must be taken into account. While the waters of the plain of Jordan were sweet and abundant, and the grass was luxuriant, and the sun shone brightly there, yet the depraved social life and unutterable abominations of Sodom were there also. The hearts of Lot and his family were human and deceitful and liable to be drawn into sin, and therein lay the danger.

The being *toward* Sodom was not safe; and safety

of soul is every man's imperative duty, and to neglect it is sinful. We have to deal with things not by themselves alone, but taken with all their surroundings and tendencies, and their possible influence, upon our own weak hearts, that are as susceptible to evil as tinder to a flaming match or powder to a spark from the flint.

When we are inclined to dangerous occupations, when indulgences and pleasures are urged upon us by those who glibly tell us that they are not harmful in themselves, we may well ask, "Is Sodom in that direction? Are they antagonistic to spirituality and a foe of earnest, active, vital piety?" If so, then it is the dictate of prudence and the part of true manhood to let them thoroughly alone. We cannot be too suspicious of evil, or watch and pray too steadfastly against it.

Chapter 6
LOT, THE WORLDLY PROFESSOR

(Continued)

WE HAVE SEEN LOT choose, and pitch his tent toward Sodom. He got at once the flattering applause of the worldly men around him. They said it was a master-stroke in finance, and he would soon be heard from among the moneyed kings of his age. He was probably a little nervous at first and had a few secret misgivings about the abounding wickedness of his new home. He had dwelt with Abram so long that he had some religious convictions, no doubt, which he did not intend to surrender. Perhaps he never wholly lost them. But one thing is certain, they became fearfully blunted even if they were not wholly obliterated.

He went to Sodom one day to sell his stock. He found it the best market in the land. And the men he met were a set of jovial good fellows, who did their best to be agreeable to him. But he so felt the awful contrast between the companionship of Abram and the vile society of the city that he could not bear the thought of going into it for a residence. Oh, no! Perish the thought! He is only going to dwell in its vicinity for the sake of the extraordinary business advantages. So he reasoned, and so men reason now; but what folly is such reasoning! We can see in Lot's career an illustration of the insidious and stealthy growth of evil. The very next time we bear of Lot he is *in* Sodom!

First he looked toward the place; then he pitched his tent in its neighborhood and dwelt in its moral atmosphere. Then he became acquainted with the bad inhabitants in business matters, heard their filthy conversation, and witnessed their evil ways. Then the temptation came a little later to move in. Business would be increased, and he would have more protection within its walls than when out on the plains. "True," he may have said to himself, "'the men of Sodom are wicked before the Lord exceedingly.' But, then, there are advantages to offset the disadvantages; besides, I can keep a little in reserve, and stand aloof from the bad society. It needn't necessarily harm me, and I must not let a small moral peril stand in the way of my business prospects."

Thus into Sodom he went, and by despising small matters of conscience, little by little he steadily let himself down to the awful moral degradation of that last night in Sodom.

So the words of the poet were verified:

"Vice is a monster of so frightful mien,
That to be hated needs but to be seen:
But seen too oft, familiar with her face,
We first despise, then pity, then embrace."

Such is the deceitfulness of sin, such the spell it gradually weaves over the soul, such its insidious growth in the heart. No one ever becomes desperately wicked all at once. Especially does no good man, no convert, no regenerated man, ever give up his good resolutions, ever backslide and fall away in a moment or an hour. Honor and character and manhood are filched from men *gradually*. There is a parley over some little thing that causes a slight twinge of conscience. That paves the way for a *worse* act, which will be performed with even *less* compunction of conscience. So virtue decays, so the heart is corrupted, so manhood oozes away, and the great fall finally comes that startles the community. But the great defalcation, the horrible crime, the moral lapse does not overtake a man suddenly, as many suppose. The path to it is not a sudden plunge over a moral precipice; it is a long path down an inclined plane, each step only a slightly descending one, but all of them together bringing a man to the depths.

This is why I am writing so earnest a message to unspiritual and worldly professors, why I warn against small infractions of the right, and inexpedient things, and evil tendencies. It is not because I am narrow and bigoted, because I feast on gloom and melancholy, and hate smiles and joy. No, nothing of the kind. It is because all human experience discloses the stealthy, treacherous, but sure and awful growth of evil in the heart from small beginnings till it culminates in the wreck of the soul.

In the warfare of earth, when a fortress is of supreme importance it is always surrounded by many lines of defense, each sweeping a wider circle than that which is within it. The enemy is always met and desperately resisted at the outer defense. So long as that can be defended the fortress is secure. So must be, and so only can be held the precious citadel of the soul. Over it floats the blood-stained banner of the cross, with the words written in living light upon it: "I write unto you that ye sin not." Outside of that is a line of defense on whose standard is inscribed: "Neither be partaker of other men's sins." Beyond that is the outermost defense, the nearest to the enemy and always the first to be attacked. On its flag is inscribed: "Abstain from all appearance of evil." So long as that first outwork is held with watching and prayer, the soul is safe. But to yield that without a struggle to the enemy is virtually to surrender all. There temptation begins with the little inducements to worldliness, and to be a traitor to duty. To be recreant there is ultimately to capitulate the heart. *"Toward Sodom"* will become *"in Sodom"* and soon be followed by "LIKE SODOM." "Evil communications corrupt good manners." Do not companion with sinners and trifle with worldliness and sport with a little sin, unless you are ready to abandon yourself to a career of wickedness, unless you are fully determined to "court destruction and embrace death."

Let Lot's life bear testimony to this truth which we are aiming to teach. As might have been expected, he became prosperous financially; for the virtue and morality and industry of very commonplace religion help a man in business. But his very success in such a place was proving his ruin. God in mercy sent him a warning. The hostile kings came and sacked Sodom and carried off Lot and his family and possessions with the rest of the booty. It was the praying Uncle Abram and his servants who rescued him and all the goods and people of the city. This ought to have taught Lot that God was with the praying Abram rather than with the wicked Sodomites. But it didn't. His attention was so taken up with business and self-advancement that he had neither time nor inclination for moral reflection. He goes back to the doomed city and plunges in once more.

He is now more popular than before, as the nephew of the man who rescued the city. We find him at the city gate in the place of office. Perhaps the enthusiastic citizens had made him judge or mayor, and his title was "Judge Lot" or "Hon. Mayor Lot"! Prosperity rolled in on him in tidal waves. He owned corner lots, and some of the best business blocks in the city. He was president of the bank, and prominent in all the big corporations, and the leader of all the great enterprises.

No doubt there was a time when fathers pointed

their boys to Lot as a model of brilliant success. He came to the city just a few years ago, a countryman of moderate means, and now he has climbed to the top. He is one of the leading financiers of his time. His wife moves in the highest circles. His sons and daughters have married into the richest families, all but two girls, who are the most popular and fashionable belles of the city. He is the man who did not let his religion get in the way of his success! He has quite eclipsed the old uncle who felt himself too good to dwell in our city, but stayed out on the plains with his altar!

This is what the world calls success, alike in Lot's time and in ours. To have the biggest tax-roll, and the highest rating in [Dun &] Bradstreet; to give the costliest swell party, and roll through the city street in the flashiest turnout; and marry children to the heirs of vast wealth, however lecherous and godless—this is getting on in the world! This is the compensation for playing fast and loose with morals and religion. The stares of the world, the jealousy of equals, the envy of those below in the social scale, and the hatred of defeated rivals—this is the climax of achievement! the object of all endeavor! the prize of worldly ambition! the shameful end of a self-centered life!

Judge not too hastily. Count not a man's life a success till you see its close. The mayor of one of our prominent cities in the North some years ago was driving in his carriage, showing two guests about the city. They saw his wealth, his grounds and his palatial home, and one of them congratulated him on his success, and thought he must be a very fortunate and happy man. The mayor suddenly turned pale, and exclaimed. "I am the unhappiest man in the city; my wife and two daughters are drunkards!"

There is a success which costs too much! We shall now see what Hon. Mr. Lot's success cost him.

Chapter 7
LOT, THE WORLDLY PROFESSOR

(Continued)

NO DOUBT LOT BEGAN to think himself success-
ful. He began to believe that a little religion
was better than a good deal more religion;
and that it was unfortunate to be too conscientious
and spiritually minded, too much given to prayer and
communion with God. But the disillusion came at
last. It came suddenly.

The last full day that ever shone on Sodom is drawing to a close. The city will see one more sunrise, but
never another sunset. The books of Lot's bank bal-
ance for the last time. The big business blocks that
bear his name close their doors for the last time. His
clerks collect the rents for the last time. Tomorrow
morning everything goes up in flames.

Two messengers appear from heaven and meet
Honorable Mayor Lot at the gate. Does something
rise in Lot's throat just then? Is he a bit curious to

know what their visit to such a place can portend? He may have seen these august personages before; but, if so, it was not here, but far away on the plain at the altar by Abram's tent.

With characteristic oriental courtesy, Lot bows to the angels and urges them to spend the night in his house, and partake of his hospitality. They reluctantly accept the invitation. It was not long before the news spread in the neighborhood that Lot was entertaining two strange-looking guests. Soon the whole street fills with a motley rabble of filthy men who demand that Lot shall surrender his guests for purposes of lust. An unreportable scene and dialogue follows. Angered because he will not violate the sacred law of hospitality, the mob turns on Lot saying, "Stand back. This one fellow came in to sojourn and he will needs be a judge: now will we deal worse with thee than with them. And they pressed sore upon the man—even Lot, and drew near to break the door." The angels had to pull Lot inside, and smite the mob with blindness to rescue him from the violence of his own fellow-citizens.

This incident was like a flash of lightning at midnight. In its lurid glare Lot got a sudden vision of his own self-abasement. He saw what a price he had paid for success in Sodom. May God help worldly professors of religion to learn from the sequel what a price they, too, are paying for their friendship with the world, and its pleasures and its success.

1. Lot forfeited the respect of his fellow-citizens. We hear a good deal in these days about going into

the world, and associating with sinners on their level in order to increase our influence over them. Men may talk as they will about preachers and deacons and elders joining lodges and clubs to increase their usefulness. It is an awful delusion—a master device of the devil.

Down deep in its heart the world despises the professor of religion who descends to its level. I have studied this matter for years as a critical observer. I have preached and done revival work in over twenty States, and I have yet to see the first minister of the gospel who did not cripple his influence rather than enhance it by this method. It is invariably with Christians now as it was with Lot. When it comes to the pinch and the crisis in the momentous hours of life, sinners show their contempt for the piety of worldly professors. Here Lot had been in the city mingling with these people twenty years, and he had not gained a convert! A jeering mob, howling at his door, attempting to do him personal violence, was the sum-total of his *large* influence for a full score of years in Sodom. *Immense influence* for God, indeed! These worldly professors are not the men who get the converts, or bring about great revivals, or lead moral reforms. No, indeed! Such things are done by the praying saints who have "come out from among them." Worldly professors are not the people for whom the godless send, when they are dying, to come and pray for them. The sinner sinking in death, all unprepared, does not care for the presence of that professor who has joined him at the card table and in the feast and the revel, and the stock exchange, but who has never spoken to him about his soul.

2. Lot had surrendered for his business success and his worldly honors, the *companionship of pure people*. As he looks into the eyes of that howling mob, frenzied with rage and disappointed lust, I can imagine him asking himself, "Was it for this that I forsook the blessed companionship of Abram, 'the friend of God,' and his pure household?" He is taking his bearings now; and it suddenly dawns on his moral vision, aroused from its torpor, that all real spiritual communion with that great soul had long ago been lost, and that he had drifted into quite another moral zone, where God was not at all in the thoughts of his companions, whose words were filthy and the imaginations of whose hearts were wholly vile. What is any possible gain of wealth compared with such a loss? What are worldly honors and titles if such a price must be paid for them? A truly godly companion is a prize worth more than all worldly treasures which have not the stamp of God upon them. Baser than the profane Esau is the man who lightly surrenders the intimacy of godly souls!

3. Lot had sacrificed all the real friends of his life for his Sodom success. Of course he had made many acquaintances in the city who used the language of friendship, but there was not a friend among them. It may well be doubted whether true friendship can be found save among God's people. The genuine fruit of friendship grows only on the "Tree of Life."

A fallen actress wrote these sad but true words: "I

was a popular actress. My face had been pictured on posters, hung in shop windows, pasted on fancy boxes and bottles. I laughed in those days, laughed at everything. Sin was gaily dressed and decked with flowers. Hand in hand I walked with her, and never noticed sorrow and remorse following close behind. "The future! It had no meaning. I would not think of it. The *present* with its youth, its beauty, its wealth, its *friends*. 'Ah, there's the rub.' FRIENDS, what are they? Why, they are the merry crowd who gather round and eat your dinners, and praise your rare china, and hold your goblets against the light to admire the color of your wine. FRIENDS! They are the people who ride with you in your carriage when you have one, and turn the other way when you walk. They are the companions who refuse you shelter and close the door in your face, knowing full well that they have shared your home with all its luxuries when you had one. FRIENDS! Why that's the word to conjure with, a word that plays more tricks than a magician, and is the Little Joker in the game of life."

That is a fair picture of Sodom's friendship in every age. It is hollow, heartless, selfish, hypocritical. When you abandon yourself to this thing called "the world," men may love you because you are rich; they may seek your acquaintance because they are ambitious; they may run after you when they wish to use your power; they applaud you, when they can get some reflected glory from your honor. But when it comes to genuine, lasting friendship which will outlive changing circumstances and fickle fortunes, that is found only among the saintly souls, followers of Him of whom it is said, "Having loved his own he loved them unto the end."

Lot abandoned the real friends of his life when he turned his back on Abram's household, and went to live with people too low and selfish and vile to know even the meaning of friendship. It was the godly family out on the plains that endangered their own lives to rescue him from captivity. It was they who prayed for him when in trouble. It was they whose influence would have helped him on in a life of piety. A great preacher has said, "I do not believe a man can be a good Christian without having godly friends."

4. Lot sacrificed his *power with God* when he reached out after Sodom's honors and Sodom's money. He probably had some at least when he knelt night and morning at Abram's altar, and joined with him in prayer to God. But he forfeited it all to gain the world. He did not even consult God when he made that fatal choice. We hear of no altar in Sodom, and no smoke of morning and evening sacrifice ascending to the sky. When Sodom's doom is resolved upon by God, it was Abram's prayers that induced God to say that He would not destroy the city if there were fifty righteous people: or, if there were forty: or, if there were thirty: or, if there were twenty: or, if there were ten. After each prayer, God said "Yes" to Abram. There he stopped making requests of God, for he thought surely that Lot had made ten converts. But he hadn't. The record says: "And it came to pass, when God overthrew the cities of the plains, that God

remembered Abram and sent Lot out of the midst of the overthrow." You see, it was Abram's character, and influence, and prayers that were respected by the Almighty. There is nothing whatever said about Lot's prayers. He may have prayed after a fashion, as many cold, worldly professors do; but long before this, his prayers had ceased to have any influence at the throne, as an intercessor for others. The poor man had lost his influence over men for good, and, what is vastly worse, he had lost his power with God. No conceivable earthly gain can ever be an adequate compensation for such a loss.

Would to God that worldly professors would think of it, and ask themselves if they have any power with the "King of kings." Are they praying, and getting answers to prayer? Is there anything more sad than to see a person, who could once kneel at the altar and pray the heavens open, and cause the fire to fall and bring things to pass, now shorn of his strength and groveling after the baubles and vanities of the world? Such a worldly minister or professor reminds one of Samson, shorn of his locks, weak like other men, miserable and blind, grinding in a prison house and making sport for his enemies, and the foes of God.

Chapter 8
LOT, THE WORLDLY PROFESSOR

(Continued)

5. LOT SACRIFICED HIS FAMILY for the sake of his worldly prosperity. No doubt this was precisely one of the leading reasons why he went to the city, to benefit his family. His wife was charmed by the style and fashion of the city. His daughters were weary of rustic simplicity, and were eager to move in the swell circles of city society. His sons were ambitious to lose their country greenness and go to the metropolis and have some adventures and see the world! Lot thought that his family would rise in the social scale and marry up in high life, if he would just lay aside his moral scruples and live in the big city. Thousands of prosperous and clean people in the country are reasoning so to-day: and they are rushing to the cities, into a society that is hollow, heartless, and rotten. The great cities are fast becoming consuming ulcers on the

body politic, eating away the vitals of the nation, its piety, its morality, and its honor.

These messengers from heaven said to Lot, "Hast thou here any besides? Son-in-law, and thy sons, and thy daughters, and whatsoever thou hast in the city, bring them out of the place: For we will destroy this place, and the Lord hath sent us to destroy it." "And Lot went out and spake unto his sons-in-law, which married his daughters and said, Up, get you out of this place; for the Lord will destroy this city. But he seemed as one that mocked unto his sons-in-law."

We can imagine poor Lot slipping out of the back door to avoid the mob at the front door, running down the alley and across the street to his sons-in-law and pounding their doors at midnight till he rouses them from sleep. They cry out from within, "Who is it? and what do you want?" He answers, "I am your father, Lot. Two messengers have come from God to destroy the city on account of its sin: hurry up and come over to the house to leave with us at daybreak."

But they only laugh at him as a crazy old man, excited by a dream. There is no enemy in the neighborhood. The night was never more fair nor the city more prosperous. The whole thing is a silly hoax. They bid the old man go home and mind his own business and leave them undisturbed to their slumber.

Lot hunts up his sons and tells them his message, but succeeds no better with them. You can see him going back home through the dark, deserted streets, weeping as if his heart would break over his fruitless efforts to save his sons and sons-in-law and married daughters. It was easy to get his children into Sodom, but he finds it impossible to get them out.

Here now is your worldly professor of such great influence. He forfeited the respect of his neighbors, his power with God, and his influence over his own children. They are enticed by Sodom, wedded to Sodom, corrupted by Sodom, and make light of his prayers and mock his entreaties for their salvation! The world has been mightier than his weak piety, and it has captured his household.

Abraham prayed that God would spare the city if there were ten righteous people in it. There were at least ten in Lot's household by actual count. Here they are, his "sons-in-law" and their wives, Lot's married daughters, making at least four: his "sons" at least two more; his two unmarried daughters, which make in all eight, and Lot and his wife. Abraham thought, surely Lot has had religious influence enough to save his own household. But he hadn't. The angels could only find four who had faith enough in God's threatening judgment to get out of the city, and they were almost dragged out. And one of them might as well have stayed, for the heart of his wife was so enamored with the wickedness of the city that she "looked back" and perished. What a comment on worldly religion! What a picture of its *influence*! That is about the average success that worldly professors have in gaining an influence over others. They do not lift the world up, but it drags them and their households down. When these worldly Christians have lived so like the world that their own children have no faith in their piety, there must be little left of their religion but a dishonored name!

I was talking once with a man on this subject in one of our smaller cities. He named the finest and most fashionable street in the city, and went over every prominent and wealthy family on the street, and of thirty-seven sons, there was not one clean and honorable man.

A famous preacher says: "I was driving with a friend one day through one of the wealthiest communities in this world. Every house was almost a palace. A man had to possess at least hundreds of thousands of dollars to live well in that community: and this gentleman told me there was not a young man in that place with whom any young lady would dare to go to an evening entertainment, much less from whom any lady would want to receive an offer of marriage—they were so terribly demoralized by this awful greed in the acquirement of gold, and the temptations connected with its possession. As we drove through the beautiful streets and he pointed to one house and another, he would speak of some skeleton that was hidden here or there, or of some corruption that was working its awful effects, until it seemed as though we were driving through the graveyard of purity and righteousness and hope." While this would not always be the case to such a degree in a community of wealth, yet it is unquestionably a fact that the acquirement and disposition of vast wealth have a most paralyzing influence on the moral and spiritual life. People become all too easily infected with the moral diseases of Sodom— pride, idleness, and impurity. All deep heart-piety is drowned in a sea of wanton excesses, and all true family life is more than likely to disappear beneath the waves.

How different it was with the family of godly Abraham. God looked down upon his family altar and said: "I know him, that he will command his children and his household after him, and they shall keep the way of the Lord, to do justice and judgment."

6. Lot lost his property. This was the very thing for which he went into Sodom. The lust for gain overruled his better judgment, corrupted his heart, and drugged his conscience. He probably at first had no time and soon had no taste for the family altar. His better self protested against the moral abominations by which he was surrounded, but those protests were drowned in the louder clamorings of his ambition for gain.

But his idol was snatched away from him. God would not let it remain untouched. It was gained at the expense of heart loyalty to God, and His displeasure was upon it all. The fires of divine indignation consumed it utterly. It may have been heaven's last effort to break the spell of the world upon him and bring him back to loyalty to his insulted God.

Woe to that worldly professor whom God allows to go on undisturbed in his worldliness. "Whom the

Lord loveth he chasteneth." If the corrupting gains are untouched, and the unholy charms are unbroken, it is more than likely that such a professor never was a real child of God; and so he is simply left to undisturbed alienation of heart.

7. Lot sacrificed his posterity in order to gain worldly prosperity. A man may sacrifice and suffer much if he knows that he is to leave behind him generations of noble descendants who will emulate his virtues, perpetuate his name and influence, and keep his memory green. This country has some honored names. The seventh generation from the Pilgrim Fathers are now on the stage of action, keeping alive and handing down names sacred to the memory of mankind. The Adams family have given two presidents and other generations of able statesmen to our nation. That great man Lyman Beecher fathered a family of authors and preachers that will make the name honored for centuries.

What about Lot's descendants? He lost them all of the first generation but two daughters who might better have died in the innocence of their infancy. They were so contaminated by the abominations of Sodom that we must drop a veil of silence over the hideous wreck of their womanhood. Out on the mountainside, the fruits of their incestuous relations with their drunken father, were born of these ruined daughters—"Moab" and "Ammon," whose descendants were the bitterest foes the children of Israel ever had! Are there in all Christendom today such bitter foes of Christ and such malignant opponents of Christianity as the children of worldly and formal professors, who gave to Christ only the second place in their affections, but yielded to mammon the place of honor? Let it ever be remembered that Robert Ingersoll was the son of an eloquent but inconsistent and unworthy preacher!

8. Lot sacrificed his own happiness for the sake of gaining earthly riches and honors. Peter tells us that "God delivered just Lot, vexed with the filthy conversation of the wicked. For that righteous man dwelling among them, in seeing and hearing vexed his righteous soul from day to day with their unlawful deeds." This is a remarkable passage of Scripture in which Lot is called "just," and "righteous." Probably both words are used with a modified meaning. Lot may have remained "just" in his business transactions, and "righteous," in the sense of being free from impurity and the "filthy" conversation of Sodom, even with all his worldliness. This is clearly possible. Men can be all that, and have very little religion.

But Lot had too much piety in his youth, had too much intimacy with Abraham and Abraham's God, to ever find much real happiness in Sodom. His ears, accustomed to the voice of prayer at the altar and conversation with angels, could never take kindly to the filthy conversation of the lecherous wretches around him. His eyes, accustomed to the purity and righteousness of Abraham's household, could never be delighted with the sight of the "unlawful deeds" of those heaven-defying people. He "vexed his righteous soul from day to day." He was vexed at his surroundings, vexed at his associates, disgusted with himself, that he had ever voluntarily assumed such demoralizing and abhorrent -relationships.

Talk not to me of the happiness of anyone who has ever been a true child of God when he is running after the world! There are secret misgivings, inward protests of soul, proddings of conscience not yet drugged into silence, troublesome memories of better things. The lips that have ever tasted with grateful affection of the cup of communion with Christ will never truly enjoy the cup of the revel. The heart that has ever been filled with hallelujahs to God will never truly thrill over any joys that come from the god of this world.

9. Last, and perhaps worst of all, Lot sacrificed himself on the altar of his worldliness. He lost the fine sensitiveness of his moral nature, his taste and his relish for pure and spiritual and heavenly things. His early aims and aspirations to be something for God and humanity died within his breast, and all his high ideals shriveled in the flames of his greed for gain. There came to him at last the darkest hour of his life, darker than that fatal last hour of Sodom when he lost his property and wife and family. It was out on the mountainside, when he came to consciousness, after two days of drunken debauchery, and reflected that he was penniless, friendless, homeless, wifeless, and infinitely worse than childless, his happiness, his good name, his reputation, his

honor, and his life all dragged down into the fathomless filth of an imperishable shame.

Ask him now if his life is a success; and he will tell you with the sob of a stricken heart that it has been an utter failure.

I was born in the Michigan woods. I have seen the fires sweep along through the forests in the spring. Sometimes they would lay hold of a green oak of giant girth and surround it with a girdle of flame, and burn it to the very summit. The tree would resist the flames and still stand; but ever after it stood with blackened trunk and leafless arms, a charred ruin. So stood Lot at the end of life in charred and ruined manhood, leaving us to mourn that a life so full of promise should have been so barren of fruit; that a morning so fair and a noon still so bright with expectation, should have ended in an afternoon so dark and an evening so hopeless from self-precipitated ruin. He learned at last from bitter experience the solemn lesson, which I pray God thousands of others may learn without it, that it does not pay to turn away from God to set one's heart upon the world.

Chapter 9
MODERN FORMS OF WORLDLINESS

W E HAVE SEEN HOW LOT'S LIFE was ruined by a choice in business affairs with an eye single to gain rather than to the glory of God. The world which seduced him was one of riches and self-indulgence, and the pride of life.

It may be profitable for us to consider some modern phases which the world assumes to draw professors of religion from their allegiance to Christ.

1. Let us notice tokens of worldliness in our churches. We may begin anywhere, it scarcely matters where. We can scarcely miss the infallible signs of a spirit hostile to the Lord of glory. For instance, take the matter of dress. There seems to be a great strife raging among the fair worshippers as to who will outrival Solomon in gorgeous apparel. Multitudes of "broken hearts" dazzling in rainbow hues and glittering with jewels! A nickel or a dime for missions, and hundreds of

dollars for personal adorning! Costly chains and diamonds, and silk and satin and velvet trains sweeping up the center aisles on a fair Sabbath, with hats and robes too fine to risk a drop of rain! Professed followers of the meek and lowly Nazarene dash up to the church door in regal turn-outs, leaving their coachmen in the street in perpetual heathenism. They carry in their hands twenty-five dollar, lace-trimmed, silk-lined, silver-mounted parasols, and wipe the sentimental tears from their eyes during worship with fifty-dollar lace handkerchiefs.

A secular paper in Toronto, Canada, some time ago had a stinging editorial on "Velvet and Sealskin Religion," in which the conclusion was reached that "modern religiosity is becoming a varnish of sanctity over the heart of worldliness." The critic declared that "if the Founder of our religion were to enter one of our influential churches today He would be shown into the back gallery."

In another secular paper which republished the Toronto editorial, appeared a detailed description of a wedding in high life where there were "millions at the altar." "Among other things which made up the dazzling display, the bride carried a beautiful prayer-book bound in vellum and ornamented with a cross, crown and anchor of diamonds, rubies and sapphires, the gift of the bridegroom's mother. The presents, which included jewels of all kinds, valuable candelabra and bric-a-brac, represented millions of dollars."

A third secular paper makes this just but cutting comment: "It may be that such things have come to be accepted in religious dress which can afford them, and that among others they excite remark only because of the wealth displayed and not because of their inconsistency with the Christian life. It may be there are those who think that jeweled prayer-books, crosses, crowns, and anchors covered with diamonds, pearls and rubies give meek and lowly characters fit for heavenly crowns and everlasting hopes. But it is hard to read the New Testament and see how anybody can think so. And it is equally difficult not to believe that a religiosity which looks complacently on such things is infected with demoralization which has struck to the heart.

"Even the pagan writers of old Rome cried out against such display. 'They wear two or three estates suspended from their ears,' said Seneca. Does the rich Christian differ from the rich pagan only in this that she carries an estate on her prayer-book instead of from her ears? They tell us, as a part of the story of the wantonness of the times, that the wife of Caligula wore at a marriage festival a set of emeralds which was worth two million dollars. Was this American bride of 'millions at the altar' trying to eclipse Lollia Paulina, 'the extravagant pagan'?"

Alas! has it come to this that American churchmembers so display themselves in the sanctuary of their Lord, that secular papers administer to them deserved rebukes, and compare them to pagans immortal for their infamous excesses?

The thoughtful minds of paganism saw in this extravagant display a fatal sign of national decay. They said it meant that Rome was tottering to her fall. And their prediction came true. Are we mistaken then, when we declare that this barbaric display of fashionable extravagance among professedly Christian people is evidence of demoralization in Christendom? Is it not a fatal sign that worldliness is consuming like a canker the heart of our piety?

Bishop R. S. Foster, of the M. E. Church, like a prophet of old, delivered himself of a "burden" some years ago in these telling words: "The Church of God is today courting the world. Its members are bringing it down to the level of the ungodly. The ball, the theater, lewd art, social luxuries with all their loose moralities, are making inroads into the sacred inclosure of the Church. As a satisfaction for all this worldliness, Christians are making a great deal of Lent and Easter, and Good Friday and church ornamentations. It is the old trick of Satan. The Jewish Church struck on that rock, the Roman Church was wrecked on it, and the Protestant Church is fast reaching the same doom. Our great dangers as we see them are assimilation to the world, neglect of the poor, substitution of the form for the fact of godliness, abandonment of discipline, a hireling ministry, an impure gospel, which summed up is *a fashionable church*."

This is what the secular editor lashed as "RELIGIOSITY"—this carrying the cross of Jesus in rarest jewels on the outside of the prayer-book instead of *in the heart;* the spending uncounted treasures in vain display, that more Christ-like souls would have given to convert the heathen world; this fashionable self-indulgence baptized with pious names and sacred emblems, drugging deluded hearts and whole congregations with a fatal opiate of worldliness as they troop on to a doom as certain as that of Sodom.

Everyone can see that the Christian Church is making no such progress as is clearly possible to her, with Holy Spirit power at her disposal. We are likely to blame infidelity or the outbreaking sins of a few leaders. But Bishop Huntington declared: "It is not scientific doubt, not atheism, not pantheism, not agnosticism, not Romanism that in our day and in this land is likely to quench the light of the gospel or re-crucify Christ. It is *proud, censorious, luxurious, church-going, hollow-hearted prosperity.*"

Another great leader in Zion says in the same strain: "It is not lying that is hurting the church, nor stealing, nor drink. It is not that sort of meanness that is hurting the church. Such church-members do not hurt us. Everybody knows they are vagabonds. If you want to know what is demoralizing and paralyzing the power of the church, I will tell you. It is this *tide of worldliness* that is sweeping over it."

Rev. J. O. Peck wrote: "Infidels are not so dangerous to the cause of Christ as *baptized worldlings masquerading in the name of religion...* The supreme want of the world today is the Bible lived. This comes by the Holy Spirit filling the soul in answer to prayer. The best defense of Christianity, the ablest book ever published in Christian evidences, the mightiest argument ever forged in support of evangelical religion, is *a consecrated soul walking in the beauty of holiness. A holy life is the one unanswerable argument in favor of Christianity.* It is an actual demonstration of its *verity.* It is an incontestable proof that Jesus Christ has power on earth to forgive sins and to cleanse from sin, and to transform character and conduct."

But such lives and such evidences of Christianity, worldliness never produces. Its underlying spirit is hostile to piety, and utterly alien to the life of the meek and lowly Jesus. Bishop Coxe wrote: "I am convinced of the perilous disposition of our times to treat our Christian duties on the basis of an experiment—as to how near we can live with an ungodly world, rather than on the principle of a walk made as close as possible with God."

Such a method of living the Christian life is always unsafe. The conditions of moral safety are greatly diminished, and the perils of soul are vastly multiplied.

This is no doubt why the good Book says:

"Love not the world, neither the things that are in the world. If any man love the world, the love of the Father is not in him." No professor of religion ever did anything more rashly imprudent than to take his habits, and customs, and fashions, and standards, and ideals from this Christ-rejecting world. "For all that is in the world, the lust of the flesh, and the lust of the eyes, and the pride of life is not of the Father, but is of the world." It is ungodly in origin, and away from God in trend and destiny!

Dr. Cuyler laments: "It is a sad fact that the members of Christ's Church have quite too often a large share of responsibility for this abominably false standard of living. I know many professed Christians who embark in this mad race for vain show and pretentious luxury. The Church of Christ is cursed with "shoddy," when it ought to put on the beautiful apparel of humility and holiness. Self-indulgence sends many a church member to the opera, to the playhouse, the party on the evening when he or she ought to be in the prayermeeting. Self-indulgence demands the superb carriage and the fineries at the expense of an empty contribution box and a starved-out piety. The canker at the core of the Church is extravagant living. And when so many of God's people aspire to live and cut a figure in Vanity Fair, what can be expected of the rest of mankind?"

Not a few people are diligently on their guard against the uprisings of sin within, who are not sufficiently watchful against the contaminations of the world that is, and necessarily must be, the foe of godliness and spirituality. Secularism is the most subtle and most dangerous foe of holiness, not so much for the gross sin it brings in, as for the God it actually leaves out. "The worldly spirit is negatively atheistic. Its plans, its culture, its pursuits, its pleasures, its ambitions, its philosophy are all godless." Worldliness is more seductive and ensnaring than coarser vices, because it is so aesthetic and refined and high-toned that it does not awaken suspicion, or offend the moral sense, or arouse the conscience by manifestations that are grossly and repulsively sinful. It enlists in its service all that is beautiful and attractive in art, all that is charming in manners; but nonetheless, by a subtle attraction, it draws away the heart from devotion to Christ. The spirit of this money-getting, self-indulgent age is against God.

Chapter 10
MODERN FORMS OF WORLDLINESS

(Continued)

THERE ARE SOME SPECIAL FORMS of worldliness in modern churches which it is not out of place to mention. It has developed, apparently, in the last fifty years. Certainly there is no trace of it in the history of the early church. I mean the modern unscriptural methods of raising money. We do not read that when the Holy Spirit told the church of Antioch to separate Barnabas and Paul for a missionary journey, the church at once advertised a Strawberry and Ice-cream Festival to get some missionary funds! That does not seem to have been the Scriptural method.

When the church is a little mutual admiration society striving to carry a select few home to the skies on "flowery beds of ease," such traffic may flourish: but when a church is all aflame with zeal for God and with enthusiasm to save the lost, however degraded and vile, something more than a *"Pumpkin Pie Social"* will be found necessary.

The men who went out as flaming evangels to move their times and shake whole continents for God, did not storm the ramparts of Satan with *popcorn balls!*

Those whom Jesus called from their fishing nets in Galilee with the promise that He would make them "fishers of men," did not repair to the upper chamber in Jerusalem to study the art of fishing jumping-jacks and doll-babies out of Japanese fish-ponds in a church parlor!

Paul never told us in any of his writings that he supplemented the weakness of the cross, of which he was not ashamed, with a *"Butterfly Social."*

When Martin Luther moistened the walls of Wartburg Castle with the breath of prayer, the answers to which changed the nations, and when John Knox was snatching Scotland from the Papacy and making his Roman Catholic Queen and her court tremble by his supplications, they were not planning "Carpet-rag Sociables" or "Broom Drill" entertainments to draw crowds and make their causes popular!

A historian tells us that Jonathan Edwards' preaching produced effects which have never been surpassed. His church became the largest Protestant society in the world. From it started a "great awakening" which extended to the remotest colony in America, to England, and to Scotland. "Edwards to this hour influences millions who never heard his name. The thing he chiefly did in his life was this: the church and the world, two hostile bodies, were beginning, as it were, to relent toward one another, to mingle. Jonathan Edwards, with his subtle feminine intellect and resolute will, threw himself between the two bodies, kept them apart, made more distinct than ever the line of demarcation, and rendered compromise between the two, perhaps, forever impossible."

But this historian did not tell us that Jonathan Edwards accomplished all this by means of "Baked-bean Festivals," and "Crazy Teas" in his church kitchen.

When the Wesleys, and Fletcher and Asbury and their coadjutors, were moving like cyclones of Holy Spirit power over England and America, bringing mighty things to pass which have not yet ceased to be, their main reliance was not "Pound Parties," and *"Mush and Milk Suppers"!* It took more reliable measures than those to revolutionize theology and Christian thought, and awaken a sleeping world!

It was not by planning a series of *Church Fairs* that Finney touched the springs of influence and set in motion revivals that have reached all lands and the islands of the sea. His work, wrought out in prayer, lives in millions of hearts, and in his deathless books, and lives again in the Salvation Army which was inspired by one of them, an army that has already girdled the earth with flaming evangels of salvation.

Is it not high time for us to set aside these church shows and frivolities and bazaars and other tomfooleries, by which this fair Bride of Christ is brought down to the level of the dime museum? Multitudes of professed Christians are putting their energies in these things which are only another form of baptized worldliness; such works will never stand the testing fires of the judgment.

The prayermeetings and classrooms that have been well-nigh emptied by these devices of the devil cannot be counted: the revivals that have been stopped or prevented by them are a legion, and the multitudes of souls they have damned only the judgment day will reveal.

Then there is the worldliness manifested in many of our church choirs. I believe in choirs, that is, choirs of the right kind. They can be had, choirs that will sing for the glory of God. I believe in pipe-organs and cabinet organs and pianos and cornets and stringed instruments. Anything and everything in the line of music that will draw the people and rescue sinners from hell. Music originated in heaven, and it is too potent an instrumentality for the devil to be allowed to monopolize.

I have been a member of a choir for years whose choir meetings opened with prayer, like any church service. I once heard Brother Torrey give out a notice like this in Moody's Church in Chicago, "We want more singers in our choirs. We demand only two requirements:

"1st. You must be a Christian; for it is as improper for a sinner to sing the gospel as it would be for an unconverted preacher to preach the gospel.

"2nd. You must be able to sing. Come first before

the Church Committee and pass an examination on your religious experience: and then appear before the Choir Committee and show that you can sing." There was a great pipe-organ and a choir of about a hundred singers in the gallery behind Torrey, and in the opposite gallery in front of him was another organ and a choir of young people and a choir of children. That church has a thousand conversions a year, about twenty-five a Sunday. There is not an organ-hating, choir-fighting church in the United States that can show such a record.

Yes, we believe in choirs of Christians, and musical instruments of every kind. But what shall we say when churches hire godless singers to sing their gospel to them, singers who, perhaps, were singing in the comic opera on Saturday night dressed in tights? The devil needs no more effective agent in a church service than a godless choir, and few things will more certainly grieve the Holy Spirit. I once sat in a famous church in Connecticut and listened to a sermon from an eminent doctor of divinity, while a quartet choir laughed and joked and played with each other, and read daily papers. A more shabby insult to the preacher, the congregation, and the God of the sanctuary I never witnessed. I challenge any congregation to have a revival while it tolerates such an infamy. No spiritual congregation would ever do it. The demand for such a thing is a sad sign of worldliness.

Another indication of this spirit of the world among professedly Christian people is the clamor for a *popular gospel.* The people in the pews literally have "itching ears" that are unwilling to hear the truth. They clamor for popular preaching of a gospel that is no gospel. "They will not endure sound doctrine, but after their own lusts shall they heap to themselves teachers, having itching ears; and they shall turn away their ears from the truth and shall be turned unto fables."

They demand that their preachers shall be silent about all popular evils and fashionable sins, and worldliness in general. The demand creates a supply, and so the old adage comes true, "Like people, like priest." The preachers come to preach what the people desire to hear, and together they fall away from God.

A doctor of divinity, father of a classmate of mine, had thus thrown himself away to tickle "the itching ears." His congregation became barren and steeped in worldliness. Among the rest his own sons were ruined spiritually. In course of time an able and earnest young minister was called to be assistant pastor. The old pastor criticized the young assistant and told him he must preach to please those rich men. A son of the old doctor said to the young minister, "You are making a fool of yourself preaching salvation by Christ. Such stuff is all out of date."

"What would you have me preach?" said the young preacher. "Oh, anything" was the reply: "preach on the philosophy of cyclones!" An emasculated ministry, unmanly, unspiritual, and sensational preaching to unrepentant and self-indulgent worldliness in the pews, is a sad characteristic of our times. A truly Spirit-filled gospel preacher, able to lead great revivals and to save a multitude of souls, is not so much in demand by our leading churches today as is an oratorical gospel trimmer, and lodge-joining society man. Hence the dearth of revivals, and the barrenness of church statistics.

Then there is the sentiment taking possession of multitudes of church-members that they are at liberty to make money by questionable and unscrupulous methods, and spend it as they please in extravagant self-indulgence. Such a spirit is utterly worldly and unchristian. A Christian businessman is as much under obligation to make and spend money for the glory of God as a preacher is to preach for His glory.

But what do we behold? Professors of religion are spending from thirty to one hundred thousand dollars a year on their pleasure yachts. A deacon once told me that his cigar bill was eight hundred dollars annually, while the entire city church of four hundred members to which he belonged did not contribute one-fifth as much to save the heathen world. Ministers indulge in this vile and filthy habit to the fullest extent of their financial and physical ability, and probably one hundred million dollars worth of tobacco is used annually in this country by church-members.

Six actresses and singers, some of them of soiled reputation, drew from the American public one million, six hundred and sixty-seven thousand dollars in one season of twenty-six weeks; and we are told that nearly one million dollars a day is spent for amusements in this country, over three hundred millions a year! It would startle us to know how much of this vast sum came from the pockets of professors of religion. This mad race of abominable extravagance and self-indulgence and vain display goes on. Meantime the heathen world is dying for want of the gospel, and the cause of righteousness goes begging for a few paltry pennies. It took Bishop Taylor months to raise the price of a little bit of a steamboat for Africa; while thirty thousand dollars change hands at a football game between two Christian (?) universities, and a pugilist wins fifty thousand dollars in a prize fight.

Thus are wasted the treasures God has given to save and bless the world. There is a floodtide of wealth flowing hellward. On its bosom float the millions of earth, wasting fortune, body, and soul. This awful waste of money is one of the damning sins of worldliness, while the opportunities were never so great to use it for God. *Extravagant self-indulgent worldliness on the part of professors of religion means* A CHURCH PARALYZED, A WORLD UNSAVED, AND A SAVIOUR CRUCIFIED AFRESH AND PUT TO AN OPEN SHAME.

Chapter 11
THE CURE OF BACKSLIDING AND WORLDLINESS

ORLDLINESS IS WORLD-LIKE-NESS. It is the direct road to backsliding. Therefore it is proper and wise to consider them together. There are two passages of Scripture which bear on this subject that are enough to make a man shudder. They are these: "Ye... adulteresses, know ye not that the friendship of the world is enmity with God? whosoever therefore will be a friend of the world is the enemy of God" (James 4:4). "Love not the world, neither the things that are in the world. If any man love the world, the love of the Father is not in him" (1 John 2:15).

1. What is meant by "THE WORLD" which it is fatal to love, and whose friendship we may not seek without endangering the soul? After mature reflection for years on this subject I believe this is a fair definition, *The habits of thought and feeling and conduct of the*

ungodly, their disposition towards God and righteousness and their fashions and customs and manner of living, taken together, constitute what is meant by the comprehensive term "THE WORLD."

The word "adulteresses" in the passage quoted from James is used figuratively. Christians in the Scriptures are regarded as the bride of Christ. Letting our love be weaned from Him and placing our affections upon *"the world"* is called in Scripture language *spiritual adultery.*

Now when Christians can adopt the business maxims and principles of the avaricious, covetous, grasping, mammon-worshippers around them, and be infected by their feverish greed of gain, they have become worldly. This is spiritual adultery against Jesus. It was this that ruined Balaam and Lot and led Judas to betray Christ. It is not improbable that this sin of Judas is the most prevalent and universal of any in the catalogue of American vices. When the followers of Christ can pattern after the world in their barbaric self-indulgence and vain display, they have become worldly. Such a spirit is utterly alien to the mind of the meek and lowly Jesus. When the professed disciples of Jesus seek the companionship of prayerless, contemptuous worldlings for pleasure, and participate heartily in amusements that are notoriously corrupting to morals and hostile to piety, and which have from time immemorial been under the ban of all devout souls, they are surely worldly, and have lost their relish for the things of God and the delights of heaven. In their present state of heart, heaven itself would bring them no joy.

This is getting to be a fatal sign of spiritual declension in some of our great historical churches. In a recent editorial a prominent Methodist editor says, "Our great city churches are Methodist no longer, either in doctrine or practice. They do not believe in the old-time revival with its broken-hearted penitents, its altar of prayer, its powerful regenerations, and its glad shouts of victory. The young people are taken into the church without even conviction, without conscious pardon. *The rising generation of Methodists attend theaters, card-parties, and dances unrebuked and undisciplined.*"

Of the truth of this grave charge I am not prepared to judge. But I am prepared to say that if it is true, it is an infallible sign that this great church is struck through and through with the fatal disease of worldliness. Those professors of religion who take more kindly to the society of sinners than they do to the fellowship of the saints and find among the foes of Christ the most congeniality and comradeship have already, like Demas, forsaken Christ and His disciples for love of this present world.

2. Why are all these forms of worldliness so dangerous and in time so fatal to the soul that God says, "He that would be a friend of the world maketh himself an enemy of God." It is because *"the world"* was and is the deadly enemy of Jesus. His purity rebuked its lust; His holiness condemned its sinfulness; His truth uncovered its falsehoods; His sincerity brought

to light its hypocrisy; His unselfish humility arraigned its self-seeking pride; and it put Him to death to get rid of Him. It would also do it again if it could, for this thing called "the world" is begotten of the devil and cannot change. The Christian believer who fully commits himself to it has simply gone over to Satan and betrayed his Lord.

3. Probably this spirit of worldliness never fully possesses a person all at once. It comes over the soul gradually, like a creeping paralysis. There is a time when loyalty to Christ has not been fully surrendered, yet the heart is worldly and the drift of the life is steadily away from God. This fact alone justifies the phrase, "a worldly Christian." But drifting too long and too far, the dividing line is crossed and the soul is Christian no longer.

4. Now "the world" is ever present and ever active. We can no more escape the pressure of its influence, than our bodies can escape the pressure of the atmosphere or the attraction of gravitation. Where then is the remedy for an unavoidable evil? Where is the protection from the malarious atmosphere of worldliness in which we must live and move so long as we dwell on earth? And if the believer is already poisoned with this malaria until the appetite for the heavenly manna of spiritual things is lost, and the delight in Jesus has well nigh departed, what is the cure? What can hold back Judas from the fatal plunge? What can keep Peter and David from backsliding? What can keep Lot and his interesting and hopeful family out of Sodom? God must have pro-

vided for His children some protection from this universal evil, some cure for this well-nigh universal disease. Blessed be His name, He has. He Himself has told us: "THIS IS THE VICTORY THAT OVERCOMETH THE WORLD, EVEN YOUR FAITH."

5. But *how* does faith overcome "the world"?

(1). Faith discloses to the eye of the soul the worth and importance of spiritual things, and so draws it away from the world by the power of a counter-attraction. This is what steadied Abraham, and kept him from going the way of Lot. Faith caught the vision of far away things beyond the bounds of time—the gleam of the "city that hath foundations, whose builder and maker is God." It enabled him to be content to be a pilgrim and a stranger, unknown to the fashionable, corrupt society of Sodom.

Faith kept Moses proof against the almost irresistible attraction of the wealth and honor and applause of men and the glory of the greatest crown of earth, and led him to cast in his lot with a race of Hebrew slaves. We can look back and see that he was supremely wise; but what but the eye of faith could see it then? He esteemed "the reproaches of Christ greater riches than the treasures of Egypt, for he had respect unto the recompense of the reward."

Faith led Paul to forget pride of birth and family, and trample under feet the honor of his nation, and be branded as a fool by his acquaintances that he might know Christ and be found in Him, and share the glories of His eternal heaven. Faith draws the soul from the pursuit of coppers to the possession of golden eagles, from shadows to substance, from the charm of sublunary baubles to the attraction of heavenly and eternal realities. By faith the drawing of temporal things is overmatched by the uplift of spiritual things, the flattery of men by the smile of God, and the attraction of "the world" by the attraction of heaven.

(2). Faith not only takes us out of the world, but it takes the world out of us. In other words, it so inflames the soul with the glory of God's character and the importance of holiness that the heart cries out for *deliverance from the inclination* to join "the world" in forgetfulness of God. It sees that all things else are of little worth compared with the indwelling of the Spirit of Christ, and it seeks from Him the baptism with the Spirit that, as it was with Paul, "the world may be crucified unto us and we unto the world."

This is the great second blessing of sanctification which is obtained by faith. It renders believers "dead to the world and its applause, to all the customs, fashions, laws, of those who hate the bumbling cross." It takes the *abnormal* out of our beings, the indwelling *proclivity* to evil, the *proneness* to "the world," the *sin-towardness* of the depraved heart. The "old man is crucified," and "the body of sin is destroyed," and the man becomes "dead to sin" and "alive unto God" and righteousness forevermore.

James Brainerd Taylor thus describes getting the blessing: "It was on April 23, 1822. Memorable day! The time and place will never be forgotten. I felt that

I needed something that I did not possess. There was a void within that must be filled, or I could not be happy. I cried to the Lord to fill me with the Holy Ghost, to *seal* me as forever His, to banish all self-ishness and pride and unbelief, to dethrone all idols, everything hostile to holiness and opposed to God's will, that holiness to the Lord might be engraven on my heart and evermore characterize my life.

"I was delightfully conscious of *giving up all* to God. I was enabled to say *Here, Lord, take me wholly; seal me now and forever Thine. 'If thou wilt, thou canst make me clean.'* Then came such emotions as I never before experienced. All was calm and tranquil, silent and solemn, and a heaven of love pervaded my soul. He came as King and took full possession of my heart, and I was enabled to say, 'I am crucified with Christ, nevertheless I live: yet not I but Christ liveth in me.' Let Him reign in me without a rival forever."

This is the blessing that will arm Peter against the taunt of the servant girl and the sneers of the by-standers. For it takes fear out of the heart, and causes the approval of Christ to weigh more in the scales of His judgment than the sneers and scorn of the world. Besides Peter will not be sitting any longer among the foes of Jesus: but he will be where he is needed, by the Master's side.

This is the blessing that will settle for Lot's wife and daughters the questions of fashion and society that vex their sex through all generations. "What will the world think of us and say of us?" All such questions for them will be swallowed up in the infinitely more important question, "What will Christ think of us?"

This is the blessing that will keep Lot out of Sodom. It will fill his soul so full of the love of Jesus that he would rather be His humble servant and wash His feet than to enjoy all the offices and honors that Sodom can ever bestow. Besides, when once cleansing grace has broken the spell of "the world" over him, he would rather lay up treasures in heaven, than here, where thieves steal and banks break and conflagrations sweep away.

This is the blessing that will cure the mad passion for extravagant display, and the spirit of self-seeking and self-indulgence; for perfect love, reigning in the heart, will lead you to seek the good of others and the glory of God. You will find your wholesome amusement in the joy of doing good. You will be as safe as you can be in a state of probation anywhere this side of the glory world. Every day will be jeweled with joys and your whole life, sane and pure, will be rich with foretastes of heaven.

---

www.ingramcontent.com/pod-product-compliance
Lightning Source LLC
Chambersburg PA
CBHW071906020426
42331CB00010B/2693